Little Treasures

Edited By Holly Sheppard

First published in Great Britain in 2019 by:

Young Writers
Remus House
Coltsfoot Drive
Peterborough
PE2 9BF
Telephone: 01733 890066
Website: www.youngwriters.co.uk

All Rights Reserved
Book Design by Ashley Janson
© Copyright Contributors 2019
SB ISBN 978-1-78988-464-7
Printed and bound in the UK by BookPrintingUK
Website: www.bookprintinguk.com
YB0401KZ

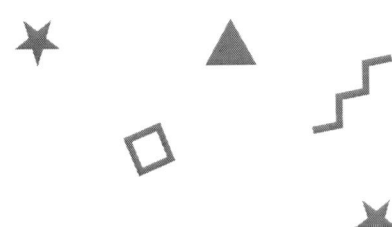

FOREWORD

Dear Reader,

Are you ready to get your thinking caps on to puzzle your way through this wonderful collection?

Young Writers are proud to introduce our new poetry competition, *My First Riddle*, designed to introduce Reception pupils to the delights of poetry. Riddles are a great way to introduce children to the use of poetic expression, including description, similes and expanded noun phrases, as well as encouraging them to 'think outside the box' by providing clues without giving the answer away immediately. Some pupils were given a series of riddle templates to choose from, giving them a framework within which to shape their ideas.

Their answers could be whatever or whoever their imaginations desired; from people to places, animals to objects, food to seasons. All of us here at Young Writers believe in the importance of inspiring young children to produce creative writing, including poetry, and we feel that seeing their own riddles in print will ignite that spark of creativity.

We hope you enjoy riddling your way through this book as much as we enjoyed reading all the entries.

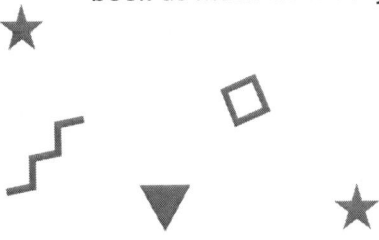

CONTENTS

Independent Entries

Senuli Welsh (6)	1
Joshua Jack Collinge (5)	2
Nathan Hunte (4)	3
Elizabeth Rosa Oliveri (4)	4
Lily Stone (4)	5
Afoma Anita Onwuokwu (9)	6
Aditya Gupta (6)	7
Ollie Pakula	8

Bearwood Primary School, Sindlesham

Holly Neville (4)	9
Leo Cooper (4)	10

Great Wakering Primary School, Great Wakering

Oliver Bassett (5)	11
Khaleesi Rose Taylor (4)	12
Isaac Mylton Clee (5)	13
Holly Anastasia Buckland (5)	14
Jake Pearson (5)	15
Darcy McDonagh (5)	16
Mollie Weston (5)	17
Poppy Mae Harwood (4)	18
Oliver Poxon (5)	19
Jesse Sheern (4)	20
Savannah-Amelie Savage (4)	21
Ava Willow Rose Giddens (5)	22
Millie Harrington (5)	23
Evie Hillier (5)	24
Nevaeh Fort (4)	25
Cordelia Whiting (4)	26

Austin Chris Holyland (5)	27
Annabelle England (5)	28
Ellis Perrin (4)	29
Amelia Smalley (5)	30
Ollie Gray (4)	31
Violet Collins (4)	32
Alexis Jane Seymour-Curtis (5)	33
Rebecca Pedder (4)	34
Vinnie Thorneycroft (4)	35
Michael Johnson (4)	36
Amelia Spivey (5)	37
Evie Murray (4)	38
Scarlett Glen (4)	39
Jake (5)	40

Heaton Park Primary School, Whitefield

Marwa Safir (4), Ebony & Michael	41
Sebastian Taylor (4) & Rohaan	42
Lola Rose Newsome (4)	43
Emalia Lattie (4), Esther & Haroon	44
Lucas Callum Delaney (5), Owen Lloyd (5) & Joe Bailey (5)	45
Tifa Langtree (4) & Owen	46
Teo Faktor Pavlac (5), Holly & Donovan Casasola (5)	47
Zak Allen-Mullen (4)	48
Michael Perrin (4)	49
Reuben Chilton (5)	50
Sulaiman Sajjad (5)	51
Abdul Wahab (5)	52

Aarik Kuc-Worthington (4), Jaxson Brandford (5), Khadija Qureshi (4) & Xavier Ajmal Eusuf-Redman (5)	53
Freddie Kerr (4)	54
Sally Ann Brooks (4), Harry Francis Linton (4) & Luke Anthony Appleby (5)	55
Suraj Alex Singh Swali (4)	56
Jeanette Tanson (5), Dominka & Abdul Qadeer (5)	57
Amelia-Paige Gifford (5) & Radin	58
Ryan Bakhshinejad (4)	59
Brayden Riley (5)	60
Louise Highland (4)	61
Shane Philip James Threlfall (5)	62
Rosie-Mae Woodcock (4)	63
Freya Dickson (5)	64
Millie-Rose Weatherilt (5) & Isabelle Burgess (4)	65

Highbury Infant School & Nursery, Hitchin

Joni Rae Elizabeth Jordan (5)	66
Harriet McKenzie (5)	67
Kieran Kealey (4)	68
Amelia Williamson (4)	69
Connor Kealey (4)	70
Katie-Louise Higginson (4)	71
Kit Trussell (4)	72
Leo Madge (5)	73
Lily Jean Flint (5)	74
Kira Donnelly (4)	75
Chloe McBain (5)	76
Joshua Smethem (4)	77
William Henry (4)	78

Holy Family Catholic Primary School, Boothstown

Louie Littlewood (4)	79
Freya Beau Buckley (4)	80
Santino Rea (4)	81
Isla Cooper (4)	82

Kayden Bebbington (5)	83
Isaac Clarke (5)	84
Harry Lee (4)	85

Rowantree School, Atherton

AJ Zulfiqur (10)	86
Curtis Brian Sherman (10)	87
Seth Thomson (11)	88
Max McMillan (11)	89
Callum Precott (11)	90

Springfield Primary School, St Saviour

Alisha Schweiger (5) & Lucas Abreu (5)	91
Holly-May McSweeny (5) & Nayara Rodrigues Macedo (4)	92
Fabian Lima (4) & Nathan Mudzi (4)	93
Sofie Przywala (4)	94
Caoimhe Langlois (5)	95
Katie Chislett (5)	96
Antiganie-Iris Sutton (5)	97
Jason Garnier (5), Jao & Ibraheem Abdullah (5)	98
Isra Choudhury (5)	99
Matthew De La Cour (5)	100
Laila Jeffroy	101
Jacob Tadier (5)	102
Keanu Ozouf (5)	103
Szymon Oliwier Duchnowski (5)	104
Tadiswa Nathaniel Mukungatu (5)	105
Riley Jay Coutanche (4)	106
Jayden Campos (5)	107
Cerina McAteer (4)	108
Caiden Gould (5)	109

St Mary's School, Jersey

Rhys Irving La Riviere (4)	110
Poppy Anna Scott (4)	111
Stanley Beddoe (5)	112

Amelie Turner (4)	113
Olly Richardson (5)	114
Albie King (4)	115
Lewis Rondel (5)	116
Kyara Vieira (4)	117
Tyler Hartshorne (4)	118
Amelie May Dubois (5)	119
Emily Le Sueur (4)	120
Maya Bowyer (4)	121
Declan Videgrain (4)	122
Phoebe Sue du Feu (4)	123
Logan Alan Le Cornu (4)	124
Jensen Paul Holley (5)	125

St Patrick's RC Primary School, Ryhope

Aidan Abbott (5)	126
Eva Efosa-Aigbo (5)	127
Maggie Moore (5)	128
Emilia Arreguin (4)	129
Lexii Gill (4)	130
Isabelle Abbott (5)	131
Frankie Burdon (4)	132
Freddie Baldassarra (4)	133
Aayan Manzur (4)	134
Harris McLaughlin (4)	135
Leo Gill (4)	136
Rania Bashir (4)	137
Patrick Morrissey (4)	138
Alex Giles (4)	139

The Mary Towerton School, Stokenchurch

Olivia McGenity (4)	140
Megan Shaw (4)	141
Aisha Nawaz (4)	142
Jya Stribling (4)	143
Gabriella O'Connor (4)	144
Leonardo Mongan (5)	145

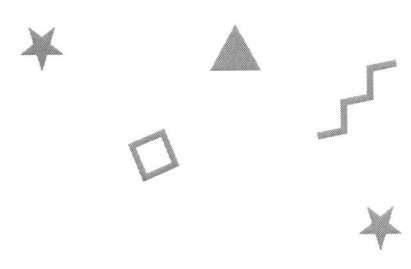

THE RIDDLES

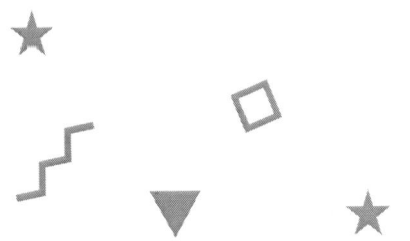

Senuli's First Riddle

This is my riddle about an amazing animal.
What could it be?
Follow the clues to see!

This animal has **fur** on its body,
And its colour is **black and white**.
This animal has **short** feet,
It likes **bamboo** to eat.
The jungle is where it lives,
Its favourite thing to do is **climb**.
This animal has **short** ears,
It makes **squeaking** sounds for you to hear.

Are you an animal whizz?
Have you guessed what it is?
It is...

Answer: A panda.

Senuli Welsh (6)

Joshua's First Riddle

This is my super first riddle.
What could it be?
Follow the clues to see!

Up in the sky is where you'll find it,
It's made out of **gold, rain and the sun**.
It is used for **making gold**,
Its colours are **red, orange, pink, green, purple, white, black and brown**.
It is a **semicircle** shape,
It has **pirates guarding treasure at the end of it**.

Have you guessed what it could be?
Look below and you will see,
It is....

Answer: A rainbow.

Joshua Jack Collinge (5)

Nathan's First Riddle

What could it be?
Follow the clues and see.

It looks like **superhero Flash in a race**.
It sounds like **a growling tiger**.
It smells like **burning rubber on the track**.
It feels like **being pulled by a thousand horses**.
It tastes like **sweet victory when you win**.

Have you guessed what it could be?
Look below and you will see,
It is...

Answer: A racing car.

Nathan Hunte (4)

Elizabeth's First Riddle

What could it be?
Follow the clues and see.

It looks like **water**.
It sounds like *pssspsss*.
It smells like **wet flowers**.
It feels **cold**.
It tastes like **clouds**.

Have you guessed what it could be?
Look below and you will see,
It is...

Answer: *Rain*.

Elizabeth Rosa Oliveri (4)

Lily's First Riddle

What could it be?
Follow the clues and see.

It looks like **a horse**.
It sounds like **'uniform'**
It smells like **shampoo**.
It feels **fluffy**.
It tastes like **honey**.

Have you guessed what it could be?
Look below and you will see,
It is...

Answer: A unicorn.

Lily Stone (4)

Afoma's First Riddle

I'm not a bird.
I'm black and white.
I live in the cold seas.
I like the cold.
I love fish.
I can swim but I can't fly.
What am I?

Answer: A penguin.

Afoma Anita Onwuokwu (9)

Aditya's First Riddle

I'm black and white.
I waddle in the snow.
I live in the southern hemisphere.
I cannot fly.
What am I?

Answer: A penguin.

Aditya Gupta (6)

Ollie's First Riddle

I have white, pointy teeth and a sharp fin.
I have sky-blue skin.
I live in the salty sea.
What am I?

Answer: A shark.

Ollie Pakula

Holly's First Riddle

What could it be?
Follow the clues and see.

It looks **red**.
It sounds like *squelch, squelch*.
It smells like **strawberries**.
It feels **wet, slobbery and super cold**.
It tastes like **yummy things**.

Have you guessed what it could be?
Look below and you will see,
It is...

Answer: *Ice cream.*

Holly Neville (4)
Bearwood Primary School, Sindlesham

Leo's First Riddle

What could it be?
Follow the clues and see.

It looks like **a long rectangle**.
It sounds like **a kettle boiling**.
It smells like **dust**.
It feels like **floating on air**.
It tastes like **cheesy crisps**.

Have you guessed what it could be?
Look below and you will see,
It is…

Answer: A train.

Leo Cooper (4)
Bearwood Primary School, Sindlesham

Oliver's First Riddle

What could it be?
Follow the clues and see.

It looks **red and shiny**.
It sounds like ***beep bop, beep bop***.
It smells like **batteries**.
It feels **hard and cold**.
It tastes **dusty**.

Have you guessed what it could be?
Look below and you will see,
It is...

Answer: A robot.

Oliver Bassett (5)
Great Wakering Primary School, Great Wakering

Khaleesi's First Riddle

What could it be?
Follow the clues and see.

It looks like it has a **spiky tail**.
It sounds like *roar, roar*.
It smells like **a cave**.
It feels **hard**.
It tastes like **people**.

Have you guessed what it could be?
Look below and you will see,
It is...

Answer: A dinosaur.

Khaleesi Rose Taylor (4)
Great Wakering Primary School, Great Wakering

Isaac's First Riddle

What could it be?
Follow the clues and see.

It looks **exciting and joyful.**
It sounds **noisy and fun.**
It smells like **chocolate cake.**
It feels like **bouncy balloons.**
It tastes like **custard doughnuts.**

Have you guessed what it could be?
Look below and you will see,
It is...

Answer: A party.

Isaac Mylton Clee (5)
Great Wakering Primary School, Great Wakering

Holly's First Riddle

What could it be?
Follow the clues and see.

It looks like **a dinosaur with wings**.
It sounds like *roar, roar.*
It smells like **dirt**.
It feels like **hot fire**.
It tastes like **dirt**.

Have you guessed what it could be?
Look below and you will see,
It is...

Answer: A dragon.

Holly Anastasia Buckland (5)
Great Wakering Primary School, Great Wakering

Jake's First Riddle

What could it be?
Follow the clues and see.

It looks like a **stripy ball**.
It sounds like *buzz*.
It smells like **honeycomb**.
It feels like **a sting**.
It tastes like **honey**.

Have you guessed what it could be?
Look below and you will see,
It is...

Answer: A *bumblebee*.

Jake Pearson (5)
Great Wakering Primary School, Great Wakering

Darcy's First Riddle

What could it be?
Follow the clues and see.

It looks **spotty and pink**.
It sounds like *flip-flap*.
It smells like **flowers**.
It feels **fluffy**.
It tastes like **fruit**.

Have you guessed what it could be?
Look below and you will see,
It is...

Answer: A **butterfly**.

Darcy McDonagh (5)
Great Wakering Primary School, Great Wakering

Mollie's First Riddle

What could it be?
Follow the clues and see.

It looks **tiny and white**.
It sounds like **a *squeak***.
It smells like **cheese**.
It feels **fluffy**.
It tastes like **spaghetti**.

Have you guessed what it could be?
Look below and you will see,
It is...

Answer: A *mouse*.

Mollie Weston (5)
Great Wakering Primary School, Great Wakering

Poppy's First Riddle

What could it be?
Follow the clues and see.

It looks like **a circle with a tail**.
It sounds like *ooo ah ah*.
It smells like **bananas**.
It feels **soft**.
It tastes **chewy**.

Have you guessed what it could be?
Look below and you will see,
It is...

Answer: A monkey.

Poppy Mae Harwood (4)
Great Wakering Primary School, Great Wakering

Oliver's First Riddle

What could it be?
Follow the clues and see.

It looks like **the white snow**.
It sounds like *rarrr*.
It smells like **the sea**.
It feels **soft**.
It tastes like **fish**.

Have you guessed what it could be?
Look below and you will see,
It is...

Answer: *A polar bear.*

Oliver Poxon (5)
Great Wakering Primary School, Great Wakering

Jesse's First Riddle

What could it be?
Follow the clues and see.

It looks **orange and black**.
It sounds like *hisss*.
It smells like **leaves**.
It feels **soft**.
It tastes like **meat**.

Have you guessed what it could be?
Look below and you will see,
It is…

Answer: A snake.

Jesse Sheern (4)
Great Wakering Primary School, Great Wakering

Savannah-Amelie's First Riddle

What could it be?
Follow the clues and see.

It looks like **a fluffy white ball**.
It sounds like *boing, boing*.
It smells like **flowers**.
It feels **soft**.
It tastes **sweet**.

Have you guessed what it could be?
Look below and you will see,
It is...

Answer: A bunny.

Savannah-Amelie Savage (4)
Great Wakering Primary School, Great Wakering

Ava's First Riddle

What could it be?
Follow the clues and see.

It looks **hairy and black**.
It sounds like **a whisper**.
It smells like **the underground**.
It feels **soft and leggy**.
It tastes like **webs**.

Have you guessed what it could be?
Look below and you will see,
It is...

Answer: A spider.

Ava Willow Rose Giddens (5)
Great Wakering Primary School, Great Wakering

Millie's First Riddle

What could it be?
Follow the clues and see.

It looks **cuddly and red**.
It sounds like *roar*.
It smells like **beauty**.
It feels **so soft**.
It tastes like **roses**.

Have you guessed what it could be?
Look below and you will see,
It is...

Answer: A Care Bear.

Millie Harrington (5)
Great Wakering Primary School, Great Wakering

Evie's First Riddle

What could it be?
Follow the clues and see.

It looks like **it has big wings**.
It sounds like **chirping**.
It smells like **butter**.
It feels **smooth**.
It tastes like **sweeties**.

Have you guessed what it could be?
Look below and you will see,
It is...

Answer: A *butterfly*.

Evie Hillier (5)
Great Wakering Primary School, Great Wakering

Nevaeh's First Riddle

What could it be?
Follow the clues and see.

It looks **pink and sparkly**.
It sounds like **glitter**.
It smells like **rainbows**.
It feels **soft**.
It tastes like **candy corn**.

Have you guessed what it could be?
Look below and you will see,
It is...

Answer: A unicorn.

Nevaeh Fort (4)
Great Wakering Primary School, Great Wakering

Cordelia's First Riddle

What could it be?
Follow the clues and see.

It looks like **a pink girl**.
It sounds like **a lovely sound**.
It smells like **perfume**.
It feels **soft**.
It tastes like **flowers**.

Have you guessed what it could be?
Look below and you will see,
It is...

Answer: A princess.

Cordelia Whiting (4)
Great Wakering Primary School, Great Wakering

Austin's First Riddle

What could it be?
Follow the clues and see.

It looks **big and green.**
It sounds like *roar.*
It smells like a **swamp.**
It feels **spiky.**
It tastes **chewy.**

Have you guessed what it could be?
Look below and you will see,
It is...

Answer: A dinosaur.

Austin Chris Holyland (5)
Great Wakering Primary School, Great Wakering

Annabelle's First Riddle

What could it be?
Follow the clues and see.

It looks like **a green meat-eater**.
It sounds like **a giant roaring**.
It smells like **dirt**.
It feels **bumpy**.
It tastes **meaty**.

Have you guessed what it could be?
Look below and you will see,
It is...

Answer: A dinosaur.

Annabelle England (5)
Great Wakering Primary School, Great Wakering

Ellis' First Riddle

What could it be?
Follow the clues and see.

It looks like **a stripy animal**.
It sounds like **a lion roaring**.
It smells like **dirt**.
It feels **fluffy**.
It tastes like **meat**.

Have you guessed what it could be?
Look below and you will see,
It is...

Answer: *A tiger.*

Ellis Perrin (4)
Great Wakering Primary School, Great Wakering

Amelia's First Riddle

What could it be?
Follow the clues and see.

It looks like **a lumpy cuboid**.
It sounds like *click, click*.
It smells like **plastic**.
It feels **hard**.
It tastes **muddy**.

Have you guessed what it could be?
Look below and you will see,
It is...

Answer: Lego.

Amelia Smalley (5)
Great Wakering Primary School, Great Wakering

Ollie's First Riddle

What could it be?
Follow the clues and see.

It looks like **a green tiger**.
It sounds like *roar*.
It smells **yucky**.
It feels **cold**.
It tastes **yucky**.

Have you guessed what it could be?
Look below and you will see,
It is...

Answer: A dinosaur.

Ollie Gray (4)
Great Wakering Primary School, Great Wakering

Violet's First Riddle

What could it be?
Follow the clues and see.

It looks like **a little girl**.
It sounds like **talking**.
It smells **plain**.
It feels like **rubber**.
It tastes like **nothing**.

Have you guessed what it could be?
Look below and you will see,
It is...

Answer: A doll.

Violet Collins (4)
Great Wakering Primary School, Great Wakering

Alexis' First Riddle

What could it be?
Follow the clues and see.

It looks **big**.
It sounds like **a trump**.
It smells like **strawberries**.
It feels **sad**.
It tastes like **yum, yum**.

Have you guessed what it could be?
Look below and you will see,
It is...

Answer: An elephant.

Alexis Jane Seymour-Curtis (5)
Great Wakering Primary School, Great Wakering

Rebecca's First Riddle

What could it be?
Follow the clues and see.

It looks like **a dolly**.
It sounds like **a lovely sound**.
It smells **lovely**.
It feels **soft**.
It tastes like **yuck**.

Have you guessed what it could be?
Look below and you will see,
It is...

Answer: A doll.

Rebecca Pedder (4)
Great Wakering Primary School, Great Wakering

Vinnie's First Riddle

What could it be?
Follow the clues and see.

It looks **yellow**.
It sounds like **metal**.
It smells like **petrol**.
It feels **hard**.
It tastes like **yuck**.

Have you guessed what it could be?
Look below and you will see,
It is...

Answer: A Transformer.

Vinnie Thorneycroft (4)
Great Wakering Primary School, Great Wakering

Michael's First Riddle

What could it be?
Follow the clues and see.

It looks **grey and fast**.
It sounds like **moo**.
It smells **fresh**.
It feels **soft**.
It tastes **sweet**.

Have you guessed what it could be?
Look below and you will see,
It is...

Answer: A horse.

Michael Johnson (4)
Great Wakering Primary School, Great Wakering

Amelia's First Riddle

What could it be?
Follow the clues and see.

It looks **pink and purple**.
It smells like **carrots**.
It feels like **soft fluff**.
It tastes like **carrots and grass**.

Have you guessed what it could be?
Look below and you will see,
It is...

Answer: A rabbit.

Amelia Spivey (5)
Great Wakering Primary School, Great Wakering

Evie's First Riddle

What could it be?
Follow the clues and see.

It looks like **a white, cold body**.
It smells like **ice cubes**.
It feels **cold**.
It tastes like **carrots**.

Have you guessed what it could be?
Look below and you will see,
It is...

Answer: A snowman.

Evie Murray (4)
Great Wakering Primary School, Great Wakering

Scarlett's First Riddle

What could it be?
Follow the clues and see.

It looks like **brown and pink**.
It smells **lovely**.
It feels **flowery**.
It tastes **fruity**.

Have you guessed what it could be?
Look below and you will see,
It is...

Answer: A *butterfly*.

Scarlett Glen (4)
Great Wakering Primary School, Great Wakering

Jake's First Riddle

What could it be?
Follow the clues and see.

It looks like **a dragon**.
It smells like **me**.
It feels **nice**.
It tastes like **yum**.

Have you guessed what it could be?
Look below and you will see,
It is...

Answer: A dinosaur.

Jake (5)
Great Wakering Primary School, Great Wakering

Our First Riddle

What could it be?
Follow the clues and see.

It looks like **white snow**.
It sounds like *splash*.
It smells **nice**.
It feels **cold and wet**.
It tastes **sweet**.

Have you guessed what it could be?
Look below and you will see,
It is...

Answer: *Milk.*

Marwa Safir (4), Ebony & Michael
Heaton Park Primary School, Whitefield

Our First Riddle

What could it be?
Follow the clues and see.

It looks like **white snow**.
It sounds like *splash*.
It smells **nice**.
It feels **cold**.
It tastes **yummy**.

Have you guessed what it could be?
Look below and you will see,
It is…

Answer: *Milk*.

Sebastian Taylor (4) & Rohaan
Heaton Park Primary School, Whitefield

Lola's First Riddle

What could it be?
Follow the clues and see.

It looks like **the end of a cap**.
It sounds like **a slurpy slug**.
It smells like **a fresh daisy**.
It feels like **a cold ice cream**.
It tastes like **a rainbow**.

Have you guessed what it could be?
Look below and you will see,
It is...

Answer: A lollipop.

Lola Rose Newsome (4)
Heaton Park Primary School, Whitefield

Our First Riddle

What could it be?
Follow the clues and see.

It looks like **a love heart**.
It sounds like **a quiet mouse**.
It smells like **sweets**.
It feels like **a bumpy ride**.
It tastes like **a milkshake**.

Have you guessed what it could be?
Look below and you will see,
It is...

Answer: A strawberry.

Emalia Lattie (4), Esther & Haroon
Heaton Park Primary School, Whitefield

Our First Riddle

What could it be?
Follow the clues and see.

It looks like **a sparkly gem**.
It sounds like **a dripping tap**.
It smells like **frogs**.
It feels like **a wet bath**.
It tastes like **a cold drink**.

Have you guessed what it could be?
Look below and you will see,
It is...

Answer: A pond.

Lucas Callum Delaney (5), Owen Lloyd (5) & Joe Bailey (5)
Heaton Park Primary School, Whitefield

Our First Riddle

What could they be?
Follow the clues and see.

They look like **snakes**.
They sound like *slurp*.
They smell like **bacon**.
They feel like **sponge**.
They taste like **egg**.

Have you guessed what they could be?
Look below and you will see,
They are...

Answer: Noodles.

Tifa Langtree (4) & Owen
Heaton Park Primary School, Whitefield

Our First Riddle

What could it be?
Follow the clues and see.

It looks like **a ball**.
It sounds like *crunch*.
It smells like **sweets**.
It feels like **a rock**.
It tastes **yummy**.

Have you guessed what it could be?
Look below and you will see,
It is...

Answer: *An apple.*

Teo Faktor Pavlac (5), Holly & Donovan Casasola (5)
Heaton Park Primary School, Whitefield

Zak's First Riddle

What could they be?
Follow the clues and see.

They look like **worms**.
They sound like *slurp*.
They smell like **mud**.
They feel like **sponge**.
They taste like **egg**.

Have you guessed what they could be?
Look below and you will see,
They are...

Answer: Noodles.

Zak Allen-Mullen (4)
Heaton Park Primary School, Whitefield

Michael's First Riddle

What could they be?
Follow the clues and see.

They look like **worms**.
They sound like *slurp*.
They smell like **bacon**.
They feel like **mud**.
They taste like **egg**.

Have you guessed what they could be?
Look below and you will see,
They are...

Answer: *Noodles*.

Michael Perrin (4)
Heaton Park Primary School, Whitefield

Reuben's First Riddle

What could it be?
Follow the clues and see.

It looks like **a ball**.
It sounds like **a slurpy slug**.
It smells like **juice**.
It feels like **a squishy ball**.
It tastes **tangy**.

Have you guessed what it could be?
Look below and you will see,
It is...

Answer: An orange.

Reuben Chilton (5)
Heaton Park Primary School, Whitefield

Sulaiman's First Riddle

What could they be?
Follow the clues and see.

They look like **worms**.
They sound like *slurp*.
They smell **delicious**.
They feel **soft**.
They taste like **food**.

Have you guessed what it could be?
Look below and you will see,
It is...

Answer: Noodles.

Sulaiman Sajjad (5)
Heaton Park Primary School, Whitefield

Abdul's First Riddle

What could they be?
Follow the clues and see.

They look like **worms**.
They sound like *slurp*.
They smell **eggy**.
They feel **squishy**.
They taste **yummy**.

Have you guessed what they could be?
Look below and you will see,
They are...

Answer: Noodles. (upside down)

Abdul Wahab (5)
Heaton Park Primary School, Whitefield

Our First Riddle

What could it be?
Follow the clues and see.

It looks like a **ball**.
It sounds like **a crack**.
It smells **stinky**.
It feels **gooey**.
It tastes **yummy**.

Have you guessed what it could be?
Look below and you will see,
It is...

Answer: **An egg**.

Aarik Kuc-Worthington (4), Jaxson Brandford (5), Khadija Qureshi (4) & Xavier Ajmal Eusuf-Redman (5)
Heaton Park Primary School, Whitefield

Freddie's First Riddle

What could it be?
Follow the clues and see.

It looks like **snakes**.
It sounds like *slurp*.
It smells like **flowers**.
It feels **squidgy**.
It tastes **yummy**.

Have you guessed what it could be?
Look below and you will see,
It is...

Answer: Noodles.

Freddie Kerr (4)
Heaton Park Primary School, Whitefield

Our First Riddle

What could they be?
Follow the clues and see.

They look **shiny**.
They sound **crunchy**.
They smell like **strawberry**.
They feel **sticky**.
They taste **sweet**.

Have you guessed what they could be?
Look below and you will see,
They are...

Answer: *Sweets.*

Sally Ann Brooks (4), Harry Francis Linton (4) & Luke Anthony Appleby (5)
Heaton Park Primary School, Whitefield

Suraj's First Riddle

What could it be?
Follow the clues and see.

It looks like **a shiny small ball**.
It sounds **slurpy**.
It smells **fresh**.
It feels **soft**.
It tastes **juicy, yum**.

Have you guessed what it could be?
Look below and you will see,
It is...

Answer: An orange.

Suraj Alex Singh Swali (4)
Heaton Park Primary School, Whitefield

Our First Riddle

What could it be?
Follow the clues and see.

It looks **round**.
It sounds like *mmm.*
It smells like **chocolate**.
It feels **spongy**.
It tastes **sweet**.

Have you guessed what it could be?
Look below and you will see,
It is...

Answer: Cake.

Jeanette Tanson (5), Dominka & Abdul Qadeer (5)
Heaton Park Primary School, Whitefield

Our First Riddle

What could it be?
Follow the clues and see.

It looks **long**.
It sounds like *slurp*.
It smells like **ketchup**.
It feels **soft**.
It tastes **yummy**.

Have you guessed what it could be?
Look below and you will see,
It is...

Answer: *A hot dog.*

Amelia-Paige Gifford (5) & Radin
Heaton Park Primary School, Whitefield

Ryan's First Riddle

What could it be?
Follow the clues and see.

It looks like **a spiky tree**.
It looks **green**.
It smells **yummy**.
It feels **wet**.
It tastes **sweet**.

Have you guessed what it could be?
Look below and you will see,
It is...

Answer: A pineapple.

Ryan Bakhshinejad (4)
Heaton Park Primary School, Whitefield

Brayden's First Riddle

What could it be?
Follow the clues and see.

It looks like **a ball**.
It sounds **slurpy**.
It smells **fresh**.
It feels **soft**.
It tastes like **an orange**.

Have you guessed what it could be?
Look below and you will see,
It is…

Answer: An orange.

Brayden Riley (5)
Heaton Park Primary School, Whitefield

Louise's First Riddle

What could it be?
Follow the clues and see.

It looks like **a love heart**.
It sounds **nice**.
It smells **sweet**.
It feels **soft**.
It tastes **yummy**.

Have you guessed what it could be?
Look below and you will see,
It is...

Answer: A strawberry.

Louise Highland (4)
Heaton Park Primary School, Whitefield

Shane's First Riddle

What could it be?
Follow the clues and see.

It looks like **candy**.
It sounds **crunchy**.
It smells **fresh**.
It feels **smooth**.
It tastes **nice**.

Have you guessed what it could be?
Look below and you will see,
It is...

Answer: An apple.

Shane Philip James Threlfall (5)
Heaton Park Primary School, Whitefield

Rosie-Mae's First Riddle

What could it be?
Follow the clues and see.

It looks like **a tyre**.
It sounds **crunchy**.
It smells **sweet**.
It feels **soft**.
It tastes **yummy**.

Have you guessed what it could be?
Look below and you will see,
It is...

Answer: *An apple.*

Rosie-Mae Woodcock (4)
Heaton Park Primary School, Whitefield

Freya's First Riddle

What could it be?
Follow the clues and see.

It looks like **a ball**.
It sounds **crunchy**.
It smells **juicy**.
It feels **hard**.
It tastes **sweet**.

Have you guessed what it could be?
Look below and you will see,
It is...

Answer: *An apple.*

Freya Dickson (5)
Heaton Park Primary School, Whitefield

Our First Riddle

What could it be?
Follow the clues and see.

It looks **round**.
It sounds **crunchy**.
It smells **fresh**.
It feels **smooth**.
It tastes **nice**.

Have you guessed what it could be?
Look below and you will see,
It is...

Answer: An apple.

Millie-Rose Weatherilt (5) & Isabelle Burgess (4)
Heaton Park Primary School, Whitefield

Joni's First Riddle

What could it be?
Follow the clues and see.

It looks like **a castle with pink icing all over**.
It sounds like **happy birthday to me**.
It smells like **delicious chocolate eclairs**.
It feels like **Spongebob Squarepants**.
It tastes like **yum yum in my tum**.

Have you guessed what it could be?
Look below and you will see,
It is...

Answer: *A birthday cake.*

Joni Rae Elizabeth Jordan (5)
Highbury Infant School & Nursery, Hitchin

Harriet's First Riddle

What could it be?
Follow the clues and see.

It looks like **a rainbow flashing by**.
It sounds like *flap-flap* and *clip-clop*.
It smells like **princesses**.
It feels like **a soft pillow**.
It tastes like **pink sugar**.

Have you guessed what it could be?
Look below and you will see,
It is...

Answer: A unicorn.

Harriet McKenzie (5)
Highbury Infant School & Nursery, Hitchin

Kieran's First Riddle

What could it be?
Follow the clues and see.

It looks like **a swimming bird**.
It sounds like *quack, quack*.
It smells like **pond water**.
It feels like **wet feathers**.
It tastes like **chicken**.

Have you guessed what it could be?
Look below and you will see,
It is...

Answer: A duck.

Kieran Kealey (4)
Highbury Infant School & Nursery, Hitchin

Amelia's First Riddle

What could it be?
Follow the clues and see.

It looks like **a colourful rocket spaceship**.
It sounds like **crunching**.
It smells like **fruit**.
It feels like **cold ice**.
It tastes like **strawberry, pineapple and lemon**.

Have you guessed what it could be?
Look below and you will see,
It is...

Answer: An ice lolly.

Amelia Williamson (4)
Highbury Infant School & Nursery, Hitchin

Connor's First Riddle

What could it be?
Follow the clues and see.

It looks like **a triangle**.
It sounds like *crunch, crunch*.
It smells like **melted cheese**.
It feels like **hot lava**.
It tastes like **a delicious meal**.

Have you guessed what it could be?
Look below and you will see,
It is...

Answer: A slice of pizza.

Connor Kealey (4)
Highbury Infant School & Nursery, Hitchin

Katie-Louise's First Riddle

What could it be?
Follow the clues and see.

It looks like **a bumpy ball**.
It sounds like **a crunchy ball**.
It smells **fruity**.
It feels like **it is rough and wet**.
It tastes **sweet and juicy**.

Have you guessed what it could be?
Look below and you will see,
It is...

Answer: An orange.

Katie-Louise Higginson (4)
Highbury Infant School & Nursery, Hitchin

Kit's First Riddle

What could it be?
Follow the clues and see.

It looks like **little brains**.
It sounds like *pop!*
It smells like **butter**.
It feels like **fluffy clouds.**
It tastes like **salt**.

Have you guessed what it could be?
Look below and you will see,
It is...

Answer: Popcorn.

Kit Trussell (4)
Highbury Infant School & Nursery, Hitchin

Leo's First Riddle

What could it be?
Follow the clues and see.

It looks like **a big house**.
It sounds like *ching, ching*.
It smells like **gunpowder**.
It feels like **bricks**.
It tastes like **dirt**.

Have you guessed what it could be?
Look below and you will see,
It is...

Answer: A castle.

Leo Madge (5)
Highbury Infant School & Nursery, Hitchin

Lily's First Riddle

What could it be?
Follow the clues and see.

It looks like **a yellow circle**.
It sounds like *crunch, crunch*.
It smells like **a potato**.
It feels **hard**.
It tastes like **potato**.

Have you guessed what it could be?
Look below and you will see,
It is…

Answer: A crisp.

Lily Jean Flint (5)
Highbury Infant School & Nursery, Hitchin

Kira's First Riddle

What could it be?
Follow the clues and see.

It looks like **a see-through circle**.
It sounds like *pop*.
It smells like **bathtime**.
It feels like **water**.
It tastes like **soap**.

Have you guessed what it could be?
Look below and you will see,
It is...

Answer: A bubble.

Kira Donnelly (4)
Highbury Infant School & Nursery, Hitchin

Chloe's First Riddle

What could it be?
Follow the clues and see.

It looks like **a black and white fish**.
It sounds like **a squeak**.
It smells **fishy**.
It feels **soft and fluffy**.
It tastes like **biscuits**.

Have you guessed what it could be?
Look below and you will see,
It is...

Answer: A penguin.

Chloe McBain (5)
Highbury Infant School & Nursery, Hitchin

Joshua's First Riddle

What could it be?
Follow the clues and see.

It looks **round**.
It sounds like ***crunch, crunch***.
It smells like **apple juice**.
It feels **soft**.
It tastes like **blackberry**.

Have you guessed what it could be?
Look below and you will see,
It is...

Answer: *A vitamin*.

Joshua Smethem (4)
Highbury Infant School & Nursery, Hitchin

William's First Riddle

What could it be?
Follow the clues and see.

It looks like **a lizard**.
It sounds like *roar!*
It smells like **smoke**.
It feels **spiky**.
It tastes like **fire**.

Have you guessed what it could be?
Look below and you will see,
It is...

Answer: A dragon.

William Henry (4)
Highbury Infant School & Nursery, Hitchin

Louie's First Riddle

I have big teeth.
I have a long tail.
I have sharp claws.
I can roar.
What am I?

Answer: A T-rex.

Louie Littlewood (4)
Holy Family Catholic Primary School, Boothstown

Freya's First Riddle

I have sharp teeth.
I have sharp claws.
I can roar.
What am I?

Answer: A tyrannosaurus rex

Freya Beau Buckley (4)
Holy Family Catholic Primary School, Boothstown

Santino's First Riddle

I have claws.
I have a tail.
I can scare people away.
What am I?

Answer: A T-rex.

Santino Rea (4)
Holy Family Catholic Primary School, Boothstown

Isla's First Riddle

I have three horns.
I have a long tail.
What am I?

Answer: A triceratops.

Isla Cooper (4)
Holy Family Catholic Primary School, Boothstown

Kayden's First Riddle

I have big horns.
I have little spikes.
What am I?

Answer: A triceratops.

Kayden Bebbington (5)
Holy Family Catholic Primary School, Boothstown

Isaac's First Riddle

I can roar.
I can stomp.
I have big teeth.
What am I?

Answer: A T-rex.

Isaac Clarke (5)
Holy Family Catholic Primary School, Boothstown

Harry's First Riddle

I have big claws.
I have a big tail.
What am I?

Answer: A T-rex.

Harry Lee (4)
Holy Family Catholic Primary School, Boothstown

AJ's First Riddle

Who could it be?
Follow the clues and see.

It looks like **an orange Pikachu**.
It sounds like a *zap*.
It smells like **an inferno**.
It feels like **a hundred volts**.
It tastes like **you're going to pass out**.

Have you guessed who it could be?
Look below and you will see,
It is...

Answer: Raichu.

AJ Zulfiqur (10)
Rowantree School, Atherton

Curtis' First Riddle

What could it be?
Follow the clues and see.

It looks like **wriggling worms**.
It sounds like *shlurp*.
It smells like **curry powder**.
It feels like **slime**.
It tastes like **the best food in the world**.

Have you guessed what it could be?
Look below and you will see,
It is...

Answer: Super Noodles.

Curtis Brian Sherman (10)
Rowantree School, Atherton

Seth's First Riddle

What could it be?
Follow the clues and see.

It looks **shiny and strong**.
It sounds like *clink, clink*.
It smells like **burning metal**.
It feels like **a shiny new car**.
It tastes like **nuts and bolts**.

Have you guessed what it could be?
Look below and you will see,
It is...

Answer: *Metal*.

Seth Thomson (11)
Rowantree School, Atherton

Max's First Riddle

What could it be?
Follow the clues and see.

It looks like **it's fuzzy and green**.
It sounds like **a funny voice**.
It smells **clean**.
It feels like **a sock on my hand**.
It tastes like **old socks**.

Have you guessed what it could be?
Look below and you will see,
It is…

Answer: Kermit the Frog.

Max McMillan (11)
Rowantree School, Atherton

Callum's First Riddle

Who could it be?
Follow the clues and see.

It looks like **an orange lizard**.
It sounds like **a crackle of fire**.
It smells like **smoke**.
It feels **hot and smooth**.
It tastes like **ash burning**.

Have you guessed who it could be?
Look below and you will see,
It is...

Answer: Charmander.

Callum Precott (11)
Rowantree School, Atherton

Our First Riddle

What could it be?
Follow the clues and see.

It looks like **a long and green banana**.
It sounds like *crunch*.
It smells like **broccoli**.
It feels **heavy and cold**.
It tastes like **broccoli and is sweet**.

Have you guessed what it could be?
Look below and you will see,
It is...

Answer: A cucumber.

Alisha Schweiger (5) & Lucas Abreu (5)
Springfield Primary School, St Saviour

Our First Riddle

What could it be?
Follow the clues and see.

It looks like **a line and is green**.
It sounds like *crunch*.
It smells **disgusting**.
It feels **cold and heavy**.
It tastes like **the garden**.

Have you guessed what it could be?
Look below and you will see,
It is...

Answer: A cucumber.

Holly-May McSweeny (5) & Nayara Rodrigues Macedo (4)
Springfield Primary School, St Saviour

Our First Riddle

What could it be?
Follow the clues and see.

It looks **green and long**.
It sounds **soft on the inside**.
It smells like **it's good to eat**.
It feels **bumpy and smooth**.
It tastes **fresh and nice**.

Have you guessed what it could be?
Look below and you will see,
It is...

Answer: A cucumber.

Fabian Lima (4) & Nathan Mudzi (4)
Springfield Primary School, St Saviour

Sofie's First Riddle

What could it be?
Follow the clues and see.

It looks like **a circle and is red**.
It sounds like *crunch*.
It smells like **sweeties**.
It feels **hard**.
It tastes **juicy**.

Have you guessed what it could be?
Look below and you will see,
It is...

Answer: An apple.

Sofie Przywala (4)
Springfield Primary School, St Saviour

Caoimhe's First Riddle

What could it be?
Follow the clues and see.

It looks **yellow and like a curly 'c'**.
It sounds like **mush**.
It smells **a bit sweet**.
It feels **smooth**.
It tastes **sweet**.

Have you guessed what it could be?
Look below and you will see,
It is...

Answer: A banana.

Caoimhe Langlois (5)
Springfield Primary School, St Saviour

Katie's First Riddle

What could it be?
Follow the clues and see.

It looks **red and round**.
It sounds like *crunch, crunch*.
It smells **sweet**.
It feels **hard and smooth**.
It tastes **juicy**.

Have you guessed what it could be?
Look below and you will see,
It is...

Answer: An apple.

Katie Chislett (5)
Springfield Primary School, St Saviour

Antiganie-Iris' First Riddle

What could it be?
Follow the clues and see.

It looks **green and long**.
It sounds like **a *crunch***.
It smells **fresh**.
It feels **hard and bumpy**.
It tastes like **yum**.

Have you guessed what it could be?
Look below and you will see,
It is...

Answer: A cucumber.

Antiganie-Iris Sutton (5)
Springfield Primary School, St Saviour

Our First Riddle

What could it be?
Follow the clues and see.

It looks like **a brown square**.
It sounds **quiet**.
It smells like **an oven**.
It feels **soft**.
It tastes like **breakfast and lunch**.

Have you guessed what it could be?
Look below and you will see,
It is...

Answer: Bread.

Jason Garnier (5), Jao & Ibraheem Abdullah (5)
Springfield Primary School, St Saviour

Isra's First Riddle

What could it be?
Follow the clues and see.

It looks **long and green**.
It sounds like *crunch*.
It smells **fresh**.
It feels **heavy**.
It tastes **fresh**.

Have you guessed what it could be?
Look below and you will see,
It is...

Answer: A cucumber.

Isra Choudhury (5)
Springfield Primary School, St Saviour

Matthew's First Riddle

What could it be?
Follow the clues and see.

It looks **orange and bumpy**.
It sounds **squishy**.
It smells like **perfume**.
It feels **rough**.
It tastes **juicy and sweet**.

Have you guessed what it could be?
Look below and you will see,
It is...

Answer: An orange.

Matthew De La Cour (5)
Springfield Primary School, St Saviour

Laila's First Riddle

What could it be?
Follow the clues and see.

It looks like **a green banana**.
It sounds **crunchy**.
It smells like **earth**.
It feels **lumpy**.
It tastes **fresh**.

Have you guessed what it could be?
Look below and you will see,
It is...

Answer: A banana.

Laila Jeffroy
Springfield Primary School, St Saviour

Jacob's First Riddle

What could it be?
Follow the clues and see.

It looks **round and orange**.
It sounds **juicy**.
It smells **yummy**.
It feels **hard and bumpy**.
It tastes like **seeds**.

Have you guessed what it could be?
Look below and you will see,
It is...

Answer: *An orange.*

Jacob Tadier (5)
Springfield Primary School, St Saviour

Keanu's First Riddle

What could it be?
Follow the clues and see.

It looks **dark red**.
It sounds **wobbly**.
It smells **sweet**.
It feels **squishy and sticky**.
It tastes like **strawberries**.

Have you guessed what it could be?
Look below and you will see,
It is...

Answer: Jam.

Keanu Ozouf (5)
Springfield Primary School, St Saviour

Szymon's First Riddle

What could it be?
Follow the clues and see.

It looks **all mixed up**.
It sounds **wobbly**.
It smells like **strawberries**.
It feels **soft and cold**.
It tastes **sweet**.

Have you guessed what it could be?
Look below and you will see,
It is...

Answer: Jam.

Szymon Oliwier Duchnowski (5)
Springfield Primary School, St Saviour

Tadiswa's First Riddle

What could it be?
Follow the clues and see.

It looks like **a square**.
It sounds **soft**.
It smells like **a bakery**.
It feels **soft**.
It tastes like **a sandwich**.

Have you guessed what it could be?
Look below and you will see,
It is...

Answer: *Bread.*

Tadiswa Nathaniel Mukungatu (5)
Springfield Primary School, St Saviour

Riley's First Riddle

What could it be?
Follow the clues and see.

It looks **yellow**.
It sounds like **squash**.
It smells like **mud**.
It feels **soft**.
It tastes **sweet**.

Have you guessed what it could be?
Look below and you will see,
It is...

Answer: A banana.

Riley Jay Coutanche (4)
Springfield Primary School, St Saviour

Jayden's First Riddle

What could it be?
Follow the clues and see.

It looks like **an orange**.
It sounds **squishy**.
It smells **fresh**.
It feels **smooth**.
It tastes **sweet**.

Have you guessed what it could be?
Look below and you will see,
It is...

Answer: An orange.

Jayden Campos (5)
Springfield Primary School, St Saviour

Cerina's First Riddle

What could it be?
Follow the clues and see.

It looks **curly**.
It sounds **soft**.
It smells like **flowers**.
It feels **hard**.
It tastes **sweet**.

Have you guessed what it could be?
Look below and you will see,
It is...

Answer: A banana.

Cerina McAteer (4)
Springfield Primary School, St Saviour

Caiden's First Riddle

What could it be?
Follow the clues and see.

It looks **round**.
It sounds **soft**.
It smells **sweet**.
It feels **soft**.
It tastes **juicy**.

Have you guessed what it could be?
Look below and you will see,
It is...

Answer: An orange.

Caiden Gould (5)
Springfield Primary School, St Saviour

Rhys' First Riddle

What could it be?
Follow the clues and see.

It looks like **it has two big claws and a big jaw with two stomping feet and a wiggling tail.**
It sounds like *raaahh!*
It smells like **snakes**.
It feels **rough like a lizard and soft like a birdy**.
It tastes like **meat! Because they eat meat**.

Have you guessed what it could be?
Look below and you will see,
It is...

Answer: A dinosaur T-rex.

Rhys Irving La Riviere (4)
St Mary's School, Jersey

Poppy's First Riddle

What could it be?
Follow the clues and see.

It looks like **orange waves**.
It sounds like *crickle, crackle*.
It smells like **burnt toast**.
It feels like **a warm blanket**.
It tastes like **hot food**.

Have you guessed what it could be?
Look below and you will see,
It is...

Answer: *The fire in our lounge.*

Poppy Anna Scott (4)
St Mary's School, Jersey

Stanley's First Riddle

What could it be?
Follow the clues and see.

It looks like **a frozen drop of water**.
It sounds like **cracking**.
It smells like **frost**.
It feels like **a frozen water carrot**.
It tastes like **an ice cube**.

Have you guessed what it could be?
Look below and you will see,
It is...

Answer: An icicle.

Stanley Beddoe (5)
St Mary's School, Jersey

Amelie's First Riddle

What could it be?
Follow the clues and see.

It looks like **two big marshmallows**.
It sounds like **crunchy crisps**.
It smells like **carrots**.
It feels **soft and cold**.
It tastes like **a Slush Puppy**.

Have you guessed what it could be?
Look below and you will see,
It is...

Answer: A snowman.

Amelie Turner (4)
St Mary's School, Jersey

Olly's First Riddle

What could it be?
Follow the clues and see.

It looks like **a man**.
It sounds like **"You can't catch me."**
It smells like **spice**.
It feels **crunchy**.
It tastes like **icing**.

Have you guessed what it could be?
Look below and you will see,
It is...

Answer: A gingerbread man.

Olly Richardson (5)
St Mary's School, Jersey

Albie's First Riddle

What could it be?
Follow the clues and see.

It looks like **three round balls**.
It sounds like **nothing**.
It smells like **nothing**.
It feels like **cold snow**.
It tastes like **cold ice**.

Have you guessed what it could be?
Look below and you will see,
It is...

Answer: A snowman.

Albie King (4)
St Mary's School, Jersey

Lewis' First Riddle

What could it be?
Follow the clues and see.

It looks like **blocks**.
It sounds like *crunch, crunch*.
It smells like *fresh snow*.
It feels like **ice**.
It tastes like **cold water**.

Have you guessed what it could be?
Look below and you will see,
It is...

Answer: An igloo.

Lewis Rondel (5)
St Mary's School, Jersey

Kyara's First Riddle

What could it be?
Follow the clues and see.

It looks like **a white sheet**.
It sounds like *crunch*.
It smells like **winter**.
It feels like **an ice bite**.
It tastes **cold**.

Have you guessed what it could be?
Look below and you will see,
It is...

Answer: Frost.

Kyara Vieira (4)
St Mary's School, Jersey

Tyler's First Riddle

Who could it be?
Follow the clues and see.

He looks **red and white**.
He sounds like **"Ho ho ho."**
He smells like **magic dust**.
He feels **soft**.
He tastes like **fire**.

Have you guessed who it could be?
Look below and you will see,
It is...

Answer: *Santa Claus.*

Tyler Hartshorne (4)
St Mary's School, Jersey

Amelie's First Riddle

What could it be?
Follow the clues and see.

It looks like **a ball of snow**.
It sounds like **silence**.
It smells like **ice**.
It feels **ice-cold**.
It tastes like **a plain ice pop**.

Have you guessed what it could be?
Look below and you will see,
It is...

Answer: A snowball.

Amelie May Dubois (5)
St Mary's School, Jersey

Emily's First Riddle

What could it be?
Follow the clues and see.

It looks **brown with four legs.**
It sounds like *mooo.*
It smells like **milk.**
It feels **soft.**
It tastes like **steak.**

Have you guessed what it could be?
Look below and you will see,
It is...

Answer: A cow.

Emily Le Sueur (4)
St Mary's School, Jersey

Maya's First Riddle

What could it be?
Follow the clues and see.

It looks like **a person**.
It sounds like **a butterfly**.
It smells like **fresh air**.
It feels like **ice**.
It tastes like **water**.

Have you guessed what it could be?
Look below and you will see,
It is...

Answer: A snow angel.

Maya Bowyer (4)
St Mary's School, Jersey

Declan's First Riddle

What could it be?
Follow the clues and see.

It looks like **berries**.
It sounds like **jolly**.
It smells like **flowers**.
It feels **spiky**.
It tastes **yucky, you can't eat it!**

Have you guessed what it could be?
Look below and you will see,
It is...

Answer: Holly.

Declan Videgrain (4)
St Mary's School, Jersey

Phoebe's First Riddle

What could it be?
Follow the clues and see.

It looks **patterned**.
It sounds like **silence**.
It smells like **snow**.
It feels like **tickles**.
It tastes **freezing cold**.

Have you guessed what it could be?
Look below and you will see,
It is...

Answer: A snowflake.

Phoebe Sue du Feu (4)
St Mary's School, Jersey

Logan's First Riddle

What could it be?
Follow the clues and see.

It looks **black and white**.
It sounds like *squawk*.
It smells like **fish**.
It feels **soft**.
It tastes **fluffy**.

Have you guessed what it could be?
Look below and you will see,
It is...

Answer: A penguin.

Logan Alan Le Cornu (4)
St Mary's School, Jersey

Jensen's First Riddle

What could it be?
Follow the clues and see.

It looks like **a mirror**.
It sounds like **a crack**.
It smells like **water**.
It feels like **a cold drink**.
It tastes **cold**.

Have you guessed what it could be?
Look below and you will see,
It is...

Answer: *Ice.*

Jensen Paul Holley (5)
St Mary's School, Jersey

Aidan's First Riddle

What could it be?
Follow the clues and see.

It looks like **a fluffy pillow**.
It sounds like *quack, quack*.
It smells like **pond weed**.
It feels like **a soft cuddly bear**.
It tastes like **bread**.

Have you guessed what it could be?
Look below and you will see,
It is…

Answer: *A duck*.

Aidan Abbott (5)
St Patrick's RC Primary School, Ryhope

Eva's First Riddle

What could it be?
Follow the clues and see.

It looks like **a feather duster**.
It sounds like *cluck, cluck*.
It smells like **scrambled eggs**.
It feels like **a soft cushion**.
It tastes like **chicken nuggets**.

Have you guessed what it could be?
Look below and you will see,
It is...

Answer: A hen.

Eva Efosa-Aigbo (5)
St Patrick's RC Primary School, Ryhope

Maggie's First Riddle

What could it be?
Follow the clues and see.

It looks like **a fluffy cloud**.
It sounds like *baa, baa*.
It smells like **a grassy field**.
It feels like **a woolly hat**.
It tastes like **a nice Sunday dinner**.

Have you guessed what it could be?
Look below and you will see,
It is...

Answer: A sheep.

Maggie Moore (5)
St Patrick's RC Primary School, Ryhope

Emilia's First Riddle

What could it be?
Follow the clues and see.

It looks like **a big pink balloon**.
It sounds like *oink, oink*.
It smells like **a muddy puddle**.
It feels like **a hairy head**.
It tastes like **a ham sandwich**.

Have you guessed what it could be?
Look below and you will see,
It is...

Answer: A pig.

Emilia Arreguin (4)
St Patrick's RC Primary School, Ryhope

Lexii's First Riddle

What could it be?
Follow the clues and see.

It looks like **a big ball of spots**.
It sounds like *moo, moo*.
It smells like **mud and yuck**.
It feels like **a bag.**
It tastes like **milk and cheese**.

Have you guessed what it could be?
Look below and you will see,
It is...

Answer: A cow.

Lexii Gill (4)
St Patrick's RC Primary School, Ryhope

Isabelle's First Riddle

What could it be?
Follow the clues and see.

It looks like **a fluffy jumper**.
It sounds like *baa, baa*.
It smells like **grass**.
It feels like **candyfloss**.
It tastes like **a Sunday dinner**.

Have you guessed what it could be?
Look below and you will see,
It is...

Answer: A sheep.

Isabelle Abbott (5)
St Patrick's RC Primary School, Ryhope

Frankie's First Riddle

What could it be?
Follow the clues and see.

It looks like **a ball of fluff**.
It sounds like *baa, baa*.
It smells like **a farm**.
It feels like **fluffy candyfloss**.
It tastes like **a chop**.

Have you guessed what it could be?
Look below and you will see,
It is…

Answer: A sheep.

Frankie Burdon (4)
St Patrick's RC Primary School, Ryhope

Freddie's First Riddle

What could it be?
Follow the clues and see.

It looks like **a ball of feathers**.
It sounds like *cluck, cluck*.
It smells like **a farm**.
It feels like **a warm coat**.
It tastes like **an egg**.

Have you guessed what it could be?
Look below and you will see,
It is...

Answer: A hen.

Freddie Baldassarra (4)
St Patrick's RC Primary School, Ryhope

Aayan's First Riddle

What could it be?
Follow the clues and see.

It looks like **a patchy blanket**.
It sounds like *moo, moo*.
It smells like **milky cheese**.
It feels **smooth**.
It tastes like **a Sunday dinner**.

Have you guessed what it could be?
Look below and you will see,
It is...

Answer: A cow.

Aayan Manzur (4)
St Patrick's RC Primary School, Ryhope

Harris' First Riddle

What could it be?
Follow the clues and see.

It looks like **a fluffy cloud**.
It sounds like **baa, baa**.
It smells like **grass**.
It feels **fluffy**.
It tastes like **a Sunday dinner**.

Have you guessed what it could be?
Look below and you will see,
It is...

Answer: A sheep.

Harris McLaughlin (4)
St Patrick's RC Primary School, Ryhope

Leo's First Riddle

What could it be?
Follow the clues and see.

It looks like **a fluffy ball**.
It sounds like *baa, baa*.
It smells like **a farm**.
It feels like **a soft hat**.
It tastes like **dinner**.

Have you guessed what it could be?
Look below and you will see,
It is...

Answer: A sheep.

Leo Gill (4)
St Patrick's RC Primary School, Ryhope

Rania's First Riddle

What could it be?
Follow the clues and see.

It looks like **a cloud**.
It sounds like *baa, baa*.
It smells like **grass**.
It feels like **a soft ball**.
It tastes like **a lamb**.

Have you guessed what it could be?
Look below and you will see,
It is...

Answer: A sheep.

Rania Bashir (4)
St Patrick's RC Primary School, Ryhope

Patrick's First Riddle

What could it be?
Follow the clues and see.

It looks like **a spotty mat**.
It sounds like *moo, moo*.
It smells like **mud**.
It feels like **warm boots**.
It tastes like **milk**.

Have you guessed what it could be?
Look below and you will see,
It is...

Answer: A cow.

Patrick Morrissey (4)
St Patrick's RC Primary School, Ryhope

Alex's First Riddle

What could it be?
Follow the clues and see.

It looks like **a pink ball**.
It sounds like ***oink, oink***.
It feels like **a mat**.
It smells like **mud**.
It tastes like **ham**.

Have you guessed what it could be?
Look below and you will see,
It is...

Answer: A pig.

Alex Giles (4)
St Patrick's RC Primary School, Ryhope

Olivia's First Riddle

This is my riddle about an amazing animal.
What could it be?
Follow the clues to see!

This animal has **fluff** on its body,
And its colour is **yellow**.
This animal has **two pointy** feet,
It likes **bread** to eat.
The pond is where it lives,
Its favourite thing to do is **splash**.
This animal has **hidden** ears,
It makes *quack, quack* sounds for you to hear.

Are you an animal whizz?
Have you guessed what it is?
It is...

Answer: A duck.

Olivia McGenity (4)
The Mary Towerton School, Stokenchurch

Megan's First Riddle

This is my riddle about an amazing animal.
What could it be?
Follow the clues to see!

This animal has **soft fur** on its body,
And its colour is **black**.
This animal has **four** feet,
It likes **hay** to eat.
The stable is where it lives,
Its favourite thing to do is **play in the fields**.
This animal has **two fluffy** ears,
It makes *neigh* sounds for you to hear.

Are you an animal whizz?
Have you guessed what it is?
It is...

Answer: A pony.

Megan Shaw (4)
The Mary Towerton School, Stokenchurch

Aisha's First Riddle

This is my riddle about an amazing animal.
What could it be?
Follow the clues to see!

This animal has **fur** on its body,
And its colour is **brown**.
This animal has **four** feet,
It likes **bananas** to eat.
The jungle is where it lives,
Its favourite thing to do is **climb trees**.
This animal has **two** ears,
It makes *ooo, ahh* sounds for you to hear.

Are you an animal whizz?
Have you guessed what it is?
It is...

Answer: A monkey.

Aisha Nawaz (4)
The Mary Towerton School, Stokenchurch

Jya's First Riddle

This is my riddle about an amazing animal.
What could it be?
Follow the clues to see!

This animal has **white wool** on its body,
And its colour is **white**.
This animal has **four black** feet,
It likes **grass** to eat.
The farm is where it lives,
Its favourite thing to do is **skip and eat**.
This animal has **two** ears,
It makes *baa* sounds for you to hear.

Are you an animal whizz?
Have you guessed what it is?
It is...

Answer: A sheep.

Jya Stribling (4)
The Mary Towerton School, Stokenchurch

Gabriella's First Riddle

This is my riddle about an amazing animal.
What could it be?
Follow the clues to see!

This animal has **fur** on its body,
And its colour is **brown**.
This animal has **four** feet,
It likes **meat** to eat.
My house is where it lives,
Its favourite thing to do is **play with string**.
This animal has **two** ears,
It makes *miaow* sounds for you to hear.

Are you an animal whizz?
Have you guessed what it is?
It is...

Answer: A cat.

Gabriella O'Connor (4)
The Mary Towerton School, Stokenchurch

Leonardo's First Riddle

This is my riddle about an amazing animal.
What could it be?
Follow the clues to see!

This animal has **fur** on its body,
And its colour is **pink.**
This animal has **four** feet,
It likes **vegetables** to eat.
The farm is where it lives,
Its favourite thing to do is **eat.**
This animal has **two pink** ears,
It makes *oink* sounds for you to hear.

Are you an animal whizz?
Have you guessed what it is?
It is...

Answer: A pig.

Leonardo Mongan (5)
The Mary Towerton School, Stokenchurch

YOUNG WRITERS INFORMATION

We hope you have enjoyed reading this book – and that you will continue to in the coming years.

If you're a young writer who enjoys reading and creative writing, or the parent of an enthusiastic poet or story writer, do visit our website www.youngwriters.co.uk. Here you will find free competitions, workshops and games, as well as recommended reads, a poetry glossary and our blog. There's lots to keep budding writers motivated to write!

If you would like to order further copies of this book, or any of our other titles, then please give us a call or order via your online account.

Young Writers
Remus House
Coltsfoot Drive
Peterborough
PE2 9BF
(01733) 890066
info@youngwriters.co.uk

Join in the conversation!
Tips, news, giveaways and much more!

YoungWritersUK   @YoungWritersCW